COVER. EBT Mikado heads toward the Sideling Hill Tunnel in this picturesque fall scene. *Philip A. Ronfor* RIGHT. EBT #18, a trim 2-8-2, blasts out of Orbisonia with a northbound freight in November, 1954. *Collection of Don Heimburger*

Colorful East Broad Top
By Mallory Hope Ferrell

Heimburger House Publishing Company
7236 W. Madison Street
Forest Park, Illinois 60130

Library of Congress
Catalog Card Number: 91-71588
ISBN 0-911581-24-3

First Edition
Printed in Canada

It is the last of its breed east of the Rockies and the oldest narrow gauge railroad in the nation. Built in the early 1870s, the East Broad Top hauled iron, coal, ore, minerals and passengers for over 83 years. The three-foot-gauge trackage twisted along a picturesque 32-mile route connecting Mount Union, Orbisonia and Robertsdale in remote and beautiful south-central Pennsylvania.

The "Eastie" earned its keep to the end of regular operations in the autumn of 1956. With the closing of the last Rockhill Coal Company mine, the EBT quietly closed its doors. It had outlived hundreds of its slim gauge counterparts across the country. In the South, the East Tennessee & Western North Carolina Railroad had abandoned its own narrow gauge in 1951. The "Tweetsie," as it was called, shared a historical link with the EBT: both had been built by Ario Pardee in the last century. Only in the Rocky Mountains and Alaska could one find a steam-powered train on a yard-wide track that had been spiked down on its original route.

The EBT connected isolated communities with the mighty Pennsylvania Railroad in Mount Union. It was here that the "narrow railroad" interchanged with the "Standard Railroad of the World," using unique three-rail trackage and its own engines equipped with dual couplers.

When the EBT wanted to send a standard gauge car down its own line, it simply changed the trucks. The slightly top-heavy car rolled down the narrow gauge on special trucks, and a coupler casting compensated for the differences in gauge and height above the rails.

When the EBT stopped hauling coal in the late 50s, it was not torn up. While waiting for scrap prices to rise, owner Nick Kovalchick and his family became interested in preserving the line. A group of Orbisonia citizens, who wanted to celebrate the settlement's bicentennial, approached the Kovalchick Salvage Company in 1960 about the possibility of reopening a portion of the line. EBT's Operating Vice President C. Roy Wilburn was still on the payroll and, after much hard work and hard cash, the EBT reopened on August 13, 1960 for tourist service over a short section of trackage that ran north out of Orbisonia. Trackage was restored to Colgate Grove the following year, and a wye track was built at the picnic grounds. Now, the rest is history.

The EBT is unique and colorful in many ways. No where else can steam locomotives be found operating over original tracks with their three-way stub switches positioned by Harp switchstands. The Orbisonia shop complex, built after the 1882 fire, is one of the most outstanding examples of steam-powered, belt-driven machinery in America.

Housed in barn-red, weathered, wooden buildings, the shops themselves are museum pieces. The 1867 stone farmhouse has served for many years as the shop's office. Hidden away in the dusty alcoves are the artifacts of railroading from another era: oil lamps, wooden patterns, steam gauges and other treasures from a time of wooden cars and iron men.

Along the old line, the rails and bridges are still in place, tunnels wait in empty silence, cars are scattered about the Mount Union yards, and a standard gauge switcher still waits in the old, two-stall enginehouse for the restoration of the entire railroad.

So much of our history has to be relived through re-creations and representation. But, the East Broad Top Railroad is not a re-creation. It *is* the past.

The EBT stands today as it did yesterday, unique in the field of historic, authentic narrow gauge railroading in the East. It is matched only by those operations over former Rio Grande trackage in Colorado and New Mexico, as well as the White Pass line in Alaska. The EBT, along with these lines, relives a time when steam-powered equipment traveled on its original trackage passing remote settings of mountains, forests, rivers and valleys.

I would like to extend a special thanks to Emery Gulash, C. Martin Miller, Miami University of Oxford, Ohio, the late Philip A. Ronfor, Lee Rainey, Joe R. Thompson, Lane Stewart and William S. Young for their contributions to this book.

For now, we must be content to view and enjoy what has been captured. This color pictorial is intended to capture the feeling of the EBT in the 50s when hefty 2-8-2s hauled coal trains from the mines near Robertsdale to Mount Union and back, trailed by a wooden combination car and admired by all those who were fortunate enough to view its passing. This, and more, is the colorful East Broad Top. I hope you enjoy the journey.

Philip A. Ronfor

Action On The EBT

The East Broad Top Railroad was pastoral trackage, meandering like a dairy cow along gently flowing creeks between Mount Union, Orbisonia and Saltillo. It then twisted, turned, tunneled uphill to the line's ultimate goal: a group of bituminous coal mines clustered near Robertsdale on the flanks of Broad Top Mountain.

Each locale had a flavor of its own. At Mount Union, the trackage was mainly three-rail to accommodate both the three-foot gauge and the standard gauge off the connecting Pennsylvania Railroad. There also was the imposing coal washing plant, the brick refractories and the timber transfer, used in later years to change the wheelsets of standard gauge cars for special narrow gauge trucks.

Sitting astride Blacklog Creek, Orbisonia was noted as the operating point of the EBT. The wooden shops that built and kept the road's equipment in good repair, along with the railroad's main depot and offices that dispatched trains in both directions, were located here.

Prior to 1953, there were two mixed trains scheduled each weekday with Extras flying white flags as needed. On Saturdays and holidays, the M-1 motorcar held down the run. On Sunday, the EBT rested. In later years, one roundtrip was scheduled each weekday, and the Brill car was used on Saturdays when the mines were shut down.

Sleepy Saltillo, at the foot of the grade, is a pretty town with an interesting station building that still stands. Nearby stood the enclosed water tank, and a wye track stood beyond it. Tracks left town on a 1.5 percent grade, which quickly became a full-blown 2.6 percent as it tunneled 830 feet through Sideling Hill near the settlement at Kimmel. At Rocky Ridge, the EBT pierced Wray's Hill with a 1,235-foot-long bore.

There were many branches of the EBT over the years, but by the 1950s, only the Narco (North American Refractories Company) Branch and the short spur of the old Shade Gap Branch remained. Only memories and abandoned grades recalled the Rocky Ridge, Coles Valley, Shade Valley, Clay Spur and Booher branches. The timber transfer at Mount Union was built to handle outbound logs from the McKelvey Brothers Lumber Company, which operated its own Shay-powered logging railroad near Orbisonia.

Robertsdale, with its stone depot, two-story Rockhill Coal Company office building and coal mines, had a character all its own. This was coal mining country, and the town reflected it. The line to the south served a string of company-owned coal mines as far as Alvan.

As long as it ran, the "Eastie" provided local color as it smoked along the 32-mile main line, looking to all the world as if it would never end.

3

East Broad Top Railroad & Coal Company's #17 prepares to leave Mount Union's dual gauge trackage for a run to the mines near Robertsdale with empty hopper cars. The fireman has steam up, as the ''pop valves'' have lifted, emitting a white plume, and the engineer looks toward the rear of the train for a signal from the conductor before he whistles off. *Philip A. Ronfor*

With a single white flag denoting an extra train, another load of East Broad Top Mountain coal steams along the Aughwick Creek Valley in February, 1956.
William S. Young

Mikado #16 smokes up the Aughwick Valley with a northbound train of coal for Mount Union. The second car in the train is a standard gauge gondola on special narrow gauge trucks in this winter scene of 1956.

EBT #17 crosses Aughwick Creek's arched concrete bridge with a southbound train, six miles out of Mount Union on November 9, 1955 as it nears Shirleysburg with a train of empty hopper cars. *Philip A. Ronfor*

Always a favorite spot for photographers was the farm road overpass between Shirleysburg and Orbisonia. Here, a southbound train of empties passes in July, 1954. The first car is a standard gauge Pennsylvania Railroad gondola bound for scrap iron loading. *William S. Young*

EBT #17 arrives at the Orbisonia depot with empty hopper cars on a beautiful autumn day in 1955. The original village of Rockhill Furnace was over a half-mile away, clustered around the iron furnaces on Blacklog Creek. The nearby borough of Orbisonia was on the opposite bank of the creek, but closer to the station. So, the railroad named the depot Orbisonia, even though Rockhill Furnace's post office was located in the station building. *Philip A. Ronfor*

Empty hopper cars, trailed by a combination car, roll through the yards at Orbisonia and past the rustic barn-red shop buildings in November, 1954. The consist is typical of EBT operations following World War II, with a mixed train flying white extra flags. In the foreground is a freshly painted and lettered three-bay hopper car.

1911
EAST BROAD TOP RAILROAD
ANNUAL TICKET

Pass Mr. J. E. Dubbs, R. A.,
Adams Express Company.

Until December 31st 19__ unless otherwise ordered.

No. 205

Not Transferable

countersigned

President

Mallory Hope Ferrell Collection

6-53 250

TIME TABLE NO. 105

The East Broad Top Railroad and Coal Company

In Effect Monday, June 22nd, 1953

Eastern Standard Time

NORTHWARD READ DOWN	No. 7 P.M.	Station No.	MAIN LINE	Distance from Mount Union	SOUTHWARD READ UP No. 8 A.M.
	2 05	33	Leave **Alvan** Arrive	33.0	
	s2 10	32	Woodvale	32.0	5 45
	s2 25	30	*Robertsdale	30.0	s5 39
	f2 33	28	Cooks		s5 30
	f2 38	25	Rocky Ridge	27.0	f5 10
	f2 45	24	Coles	25.0	f5 00
	f2 48	23	Kimmel	24.0	f4 55
	f2 52	22	Fairview	23.0	f4 50
	s3 06	19	*Saltillo	22.0	f4 45
	s3 12	17	Three Springs	19.0	s4 30
	f3 22	14	Pogue	17.0	s4 20
	3 35	11	Arrive Leave *Orbisonia Leave Arrive	14.0	f4 10
		7		11.0	4 00
		5	Shirleysburg		
		4	Pump Station	7.0	
			Aughwick	5.0	
			Adams	4.0	
		1	Allenport	2.4	
			*Mount Union Yard	1.0	
		0	Arrive *Mt. Union Leave	.4	
				.0	

s—Regular Stop. f—Stop on signal. *Train order stations.

Operates Days Mines Are Working Only

RESPONSIBILITY—The East Broad Top Railroad and Coal Company is not responsible for errors in time tables, nor for inconvenience or damage resulting from delayed trains or failure to make connections, or for shortage of equipment. The schedules and equipment shown in this time table are subject to change without notice.

RAILWAY EXPRESS SHIPMENTS MOVE VIA HIGHWAY TRUCK OF THIS COMPANY DAILY EXCEPT SUNDAY

Telephones—Orbisonia 211, Mount Union 126 and 127

C. R. WILBURN, Operating Vice President

Mallory Hope Ferrell Collection

EBT #16 leads a train of empty southbound hoppers between Orbisonia and Pogue on December 5, 1955. The trees show off the last of their autumn leaves, and the fields have been cut and await winter, which is only days away. *Philip A. Ronfor*

EBT #16 heads northbound across the Aughwick Creek trestle near Pogue in the summer of 1955. Foliage obscures part of the trestle, which was the longest crossing on the EBT.

Mikado #18 nears Pogue in the autumn of 1954. The cobalt-blue sky provides a fine background for the southbound freight that heads into the late afternoon sun.

EBT #18, a 2-8-2, heads south for Robertsdale with a long string of hopper cars, blasting through Three Springs at Milepost 17.0 in November, 1954. The Baldwin-built Mikado was the last narrow gauge engine constructed for the EBT. It was outshopped in 1920.

A northbound mixed train pauses at the Saltillo depot in the fall of 1954. The Pullman-green combination car was typical of the last years and preferred by crews for its riding quality and additional room for less-than-carload freight. The picturesque town of Saltillo (pronounced locally Sal-til-o) was a source of local traffic for the EBT, and overnight guests were accommodated at Hotel La Palace, across the street from the depot.

ABOVE. EBT #17 approaches the enclosed water tank at Saltillo from the south. INSERT. The fireman fills the 2-8-2's tender at the rustic red structure. The enclosure protected the water tank from freezing, and a stove provided additional heat during cold weather. *Philip A. Ronfor*

EBT #17 pauses at the water tank on a beautiful and colorful autumn afternoon before heading north to Orbisonia and Mount Union with its loaded hoppers.
Philip A. Ronfor

EBT #17 works a loaded train out of Saltillo on November 9, 1955. In the consist of loaded hopper cars are several cars with rebuilt sideboards, which increased the carrying capacity by an additional 10 tons of coal. In the background are carloads of ganister rock from the steep Narco Spur. *Philip A. Ronfor*

EBT #18, last of the EBT Mikados, moves loads through Saltillo in this November, 1954 scene, which was photographed south of the depot and main street crossing. The weathered water tank is in the background, and the Saltillo wye track was located beyond the water tank and creek crossing.

EBT #17 pushes a short string of hopper cars up the steep Narco Branch. The line was constructed in 1942, 2.44 miles near Saltillo, in order to serve one of the North American Refractories Company's ganister rock quarries. *Philip A. Ronfor*

The Narco Branch was both steep and short, with the grade reaching three percent. Locomotives were kept on the downhill end of trains. Philip Ronfor found #17 on the branch in November, 1955. Following the abandonment of the EBT in 1956, the Narco Branch was one of the few pieces of trackage removed.

LEFT. The beautiful fall colors abound as 2-8-2 #17 swings its train of northbound coal around the curve at Kimmel before entering the Sideling Hill Tunnel on November 9, 1955. ABOVE. Trailing the consist was the typical combination car that was favored by train crews over the EBT's caboose cars. *Philip A. Ronfor*

EBT #18 heads a northbound coal drag at Kimmel in 1954. The cast iron, oval railroad crossing sign was common on the EBT as well as other lines in Pennsylvania.

EBT #18 blasts out of Sideling Hill Tunnel near Kimmel. The 830-foot-long tunnel was located in the center of a 17-degree curve, one of the sharpest on the road. The north portals to both EBT tunnels were protected by automatic doors to prevent ice from forming on the rails in winter.

ABOVE. Mikado #14 emerges from the north portal of Sideling Hill Tunnel in 1956. *Philip A. Ronfor* RIGHT. EBT #17 comes out of Wray's Hill Tunnel near Rocky Ridge. The north portal of Sideling Hill Tunnel as well as both entrances to the Wray's Hill bore were equipped with electrically operated doors to prevent ice from forming inside the tunnels. *Philip A. Ronfor*

EBT #18 pauses at the Robertsdale water tank in the fall of 1954. At left is the loading ramp for the Rockhill Iron & Coal Company's No. 5 mine, known by locals as "The Slope."

ABOVE. EBT #15 makes up a train of loaded hoppers before turning on the wye track at Robertsdale. The Rockhill Iron & Coal Company Office and the Robertsdale post office are visible in the background. Robertsdale is named for Robert and Percival Roberts, who found coal on nearby Broad Top Mountain in 1855. LEFT. EBT #15 takes water at the Woodvale water tank at Milepost 32.0, near the end of the line, in March, 1956. *Philip A. Ronfor*

EBT #17 and crew turn the engine, box car and combination car #15 on the Robertsdale wye track on March 23, 1956 before heading back to Orbisonia. The tail of the wye crossed Trough Creek, and the switches were controlled by ancient Harp switchstands. *Philip A. Ronfor*

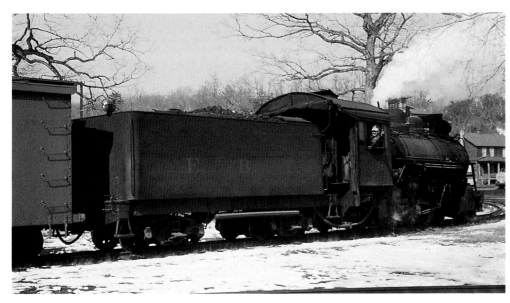

EBT #17 backs around the Robertsdale wye track with a box car of company material and combination car #15 on March 23, 1956. At the time these photographs were taken, the abandonment notices already had been posted on station doors along the line, and the final run was made two weeks later on April 6, 1956. *Philip A. Ronfor*

Mount Union was the point where the narrow gauge met the Pennsylvania's "Standard Railroad of the World." Looking north, narrow gauge, standard gauge and dual gauge trackage is visible. This 1954 view also shows the giant sand flotation plant and the timber transfer. On the right side of the photograph in the background, the North American Refractories plant can be seen.

Three-rail trackage abounds in the Mount Union yards. The EBT did the switching with its own standard gauge switchers, which were equipped with dual couplers. At the right of this scene are spare narrow gauge trucks used under standard gauge cars when these cars ventured onto the three-foot-gauge EBT.

This rare three-way stub switch, controlled by a Harp switchstand, was located in the Mount Union yards near the coal washing plant. It is unusual in that it is standard gauge. Similar narrow gauge three-way stub switches still are used at Orbisonia.

The EBT's timber transfer was originally constructed to transfer logs and props from narrow gauge cars to standard gauge cars, which were mainly used by the McKelvey Brothers Lumber Company that had a Shay-powered logging line on Blacklog Mountain. Built in the early 1920s, the gantry crane timber transfer was out of service by 1928 when McKelvey Brothers removed its line. In 1933, the EBT began using the crane to transfer the trucks from standard gauge cars to special narrow gauge trucks for trips over the slim gauge trackage. The simple arrangement worked and added to the longevity of the EBT.

This is a view of the EBT railroad yards in 1956 looking north. A wooden box car serves as a storage shed, and the timber transfer and sand flotation plant are visible in the distance.

The sand flotation plant was located in the center of the Mount Union yards. Mined coal had to be off-loaded from the narrow gauge and into the washing plant, while outbound coal was loaded into standard gauge equipment. The so-called ''break in gauge'' or transfer of goods was not the major economic factor for the EBT as it was for some other narrow gauge lines.

The Mount Union enginehouse, with its nearby enclosed water tank, was located at the north end of the EBT's yard. The two-stall house normally housed the standard gauge switch engine and narrow gauge engines that tied up there. This is how it looked in the final year of operations in 1956.

Near the Mount Union enginehouse was the transfer shed, used for LCL freight that needed to be moved from one gauge to the other. This facility saw little use in later years, but was available, if needed.

The Mount Union enginehouse was built of blocks and contained two three-rail tracks. Decades after the EBT stopped hauling coal to Mount Union, 0-6-0 #3 is still stored inside the enginehouse, although small trees now grow between the rails.

The EBT connected with the giant Pennsylvania Railroad on Pennsylvania Street in Mount Union. The Pennsylvania Railroad tracks reached here in June, 1850; the EBT started here in 1872. The Pennsylvania Railroad tracks were later moved further north to avoid main line service on the town streets.

The EBT's shop area in Orbisonia is a delight to behold. Its old, barn-red wooden buildings and original stone office building are seen through the roundhouse door. Many of the shop buildings date from the early 1880s and are filled with over a century of narrow gauge artifacts and historic machinery. This scene was photographed in June, 1955 and shows #16 on the turntable.

The Orbisonia shop office is housed in an 1867 farmhouse that was part of the original land purchased for the terminal. The first shops were built during 1873-74. A fire destroyed them in 1882.

EBT #16 prepares to go to work on a rainy day in June, 1955. In the background are the familiar twin stacks of the shop building, powered for many years by a huge, stationary steam engine that was moved there from the iron furnace following the 1882 fire.

The eight-stall Orbisonia roundhouse was constructed of bricks, and the turntable was built by Strobel Steel of Chicago from an 1884 patent. It is shown here in 1956.

The EBT's paint shop, located next to the roundhouse in Orbisonia, was of brick construction. The original village of Rockhill Furnace was located near the iron furnace on Blacklog Creek, some distance from the shop complex. Over the years, the settlement of Rockhill Furnace slowly built around the EBT's depot, which the railroad named Orbisonia after the borough that was located across Jordan Creek, but closer to the shops and station.

44

Harp switchstands and stub switches were once common in 19th Century American railroading, but are quite rare today. This one was located behind the EBT's shop. The 1867 farmhouse and its "add-on" storage buildings are at the left, while the rear of the shop is at the right. The switch leads to the turntable (left) and main line (right).

In this view behind the shops, the sand house (left) and old farmhouse can be seen, with the rear of the boiler shop at the right. The weed-grown siding at the left leads to the paint shop, which is visible in the distance.

The EBT constructed many of its own cars at the Orbisonia car shops. The wooden shop buildings were painted a rustic, barn-red color. When the weather permitted, the car men preferred to rivet the huge iron sheets that formed the hopper cars outside the shop. The twin stacks rise from the corner of the machine shop, which was attached to the car shop. *Emery Gulash*

The freight office was located across the tracks from the Orbisonia depot and on the south side of Meadow Street. As this 1956 photograph attests, the freight office saw little activity in later years.

The coaling ramp, with its steeply graded trackage, served EBT locomotives at Orbisonia along with the standpipe that provided water for the engines. They were located near the southern end of the yards and still see service. This view shows the layout in 1955.

The Orbisonia depot was built in 1906. It contained offices on the second floor for the general manager and the chief dispatcher, who could look out of his bay window to see the action. The Rockhill Furnace post office occupied a corner of the first floor, along with the waiting room for passengers.

This view shows the southern end of the Orbisonia yards as they were in the mid-1950s. The three-way stub switch is activated by a historic Harp switchstand, and the coaling pocket is in the background. Note that on a stub switch, the rails actually bend. Even today, railroad switchmen are referred to as "rail benders."

Even a narrow gauge railroad like the EBT required some standard gauge motive power to switch the complex yards at Mount Union. In the post-World War II era, the job was handled by a pair of 0-6-0 switchers, #3 and #6. The 3 spot is under steam at the enginehouse in the summer of 1955. It is Baldwin #56325, which was built in 1923. Notice that it sports a full-size automatic coupler as well as three-quarter-size couplers for narrow gauge equipment.

Smoke Up The Valley

The EBT was a well-maintained shortline. Its engines were kept painted with yellow-orange lettering proudly proclaiming their ownership. They were built by the Baldwin Locomotive Works in Philadelphia. Beginning in 1911, the railroad acquired the first of six 2-8-2 Mikado-type locomotives. The fact that all six are still on the property attests to the workmanship of both the builder and the EBT's shopmen.

The EBT was the first narrow gauge line to use all-steel cars, which were originally constructed by the Pressed Steel Car Company. The Orbisonia shop began building its own steel hopper cars by 1914. Over the years, the shops rebuilt many of the cars from two-bay and three-bay hopper cars and increased the capacity with the addition of higher sideboards on others. The shop also produced box cars, flat cars, tank cars, cabooses and other homebuilts as needed. The shops put together the M-1 motorcar in 1927 using parts from J.G. Brill and Westinghouse. The bulk of the rolling stock was the fleet of black-painted hopper cars, riding on Vulcan trucks and sporting the EBT's own herald. After 1904, the EBT's equipment used three-quarter-size Master Car Builder's automatic couplers.

By the 1950s, most of the line's earlier wooden freight equipment was retired. The wooden passenger cars remained from the beginning of the line in 1872 until the present. Many members of this varnish fleet were acquired secondhand from other roads, notably the Boston, Revere Beach & Lynn Railroad. The beautiful business car *Orbisonia* came from the Bradford, Bordell & Kinzua Railroad via the Big Level & Kinzua, two other Pennsylvania slim gauge pikes.

The EBT had a small fleet of standard gauge cars and locomotives that were confined to the Mount Union yards. A pair of 0-6-0s saw service in the final

The other Mount Union switcher was #6, an 0-6-0 that was built by Baldwin (#30046) in 1907. It is pictured in the yards on the enginehouse lead track in 1952.

decades, and #3 is still locked in the two-stall enginehouse, although six- to eight-inch-thick trees now grow between the weed-covered rails.

The Mikados continued as the mainstay motive power of the EBT from World War I until 1956. Numbered #12 through #18 (there was no #13), each 2-8-2 was a bit heavier than the previous one. As Engineer Frank Rinker said, ''They are darn good engines.''

Beginning in 1911, the EBT purchased the first of six Baldwin 2-8-2 Mikado-type locomotives. EBT #12 was the first of what became the line's mainstay motive power. It was Baldwin #37325; it sported slide valves, as did #14 and #15. The 12 spot derailed in Sideling Hill Tunnel due to ice on the rails on its first trip. *Joe R. Thompson*

Following the success of the first 2-8-2 #12, the EBT ordered others, which were delivered from the Baldwin Locomotive Works at two-year intervals, starting with #14 (Baldwin #38625) that arrived in 1912. Each Mikado was slightly heavier than the previous one. EBT #14 is seen here at Orbisonia in the summer of 1954. *William S. Young*

EBT #15, a 2-8-2, arrived in 1914 from the Baldwin Locomotive Works (#41196). It served the line for over four decades, and it still sees service. EBT #15 is seen at Robertsdale in 1955. *Philip A. Ronfor*

EBT #16 arrived on the EBT in 1916 (Baldwin #43562) and is pictured near the Orbisonia roundhouse with a train of empties in 1952. Notice the #16 sports piston valves and a rare use of the Southern valve gear that was applied to #16, #17 and #18.

EBT #15 is seen at Robertsdale in November, 1954. The station building is in the background with the loading tipple for the No. 1 mine at the left of the scene.

EBT #17 arrived from Baldwin (#48075) in 1918. Like #16 that arrived two years earlier, it had piston valves and Southern valve gear. It pauses while the engineer "oils around" at Saltillo water tank on November 9, 1955. *Philip A. Ronfor*

The last of its breed on the EBT was 2-8-2 #18, which arrived from Baldwin (#53541) in the fall of 1920. It was the largest and last of the EBT's 2-8-2 fleet with a total engine weight of 164,200 pounds. It prepares to leave Mount Union on a frosty winter morning in 1954.

Passenger Cars

In later years, after the EBT stopped operating passenger trains, the daily mixed trains were trailed by either a red caboose or a green combination car. Crewmen preferred the combination cars because they traveled better, and they had more room for LCL cargo and the occasional passenger who wanted to ride. Combination car #14 came to the EBT from the Boston, Revere Beach & Lynn and is seen in the Orbisonia yards in 1955.
Philip A. Ronfor

Combination car #14 was frequently used in the post-World War II period at the end of EBT trains. As rebuilt by the EBT, it seated 14 passengers, but seldom carried more than the conductor and two brakemen. It is pictured at Orbisonia on February 13, 1956 shortly before the end of operations in April.

Most of the passenger equipment during the later years of operation was secondhand, but combination car #18 was one of the few surviving cars that was originally built for the EBT. EBT #18 is at Orbisonia, painted and ready for sale in February, 1956. It was sold to a never-built tourist operation in Michigan and, today, it is privately owned and in poor condition in Colorado.

Combination car #18 is seen here at Orbisonia in the summer of 1954. It had been used as the payroll car for many years, and had iron bars over the windows of the baggage section to attest to that. *William S. Young*

Combination car #29, shown in work car red paint, was bought secondhand from the Au Sable & Northwestern in 1916 and was sold to the Northwoods (tourist) line in 1956. The Michigan tourist line was never built, and #29 is now privately owned at Fort Lupton, Colorado. In regular EBT service, it was used on the ''mail train.'' This scene was photographed in the summer of 1955 at Orbisonia.

Business car #20 was named the *Orbisonia* and was acquired from the Big Level & Kinzua, another Pennsylvania narrow gauge line. The car was built by the Billmeyer & Small Car Works of York, Pennsylvania, which was a major builder of equipment for narrow gauge roads.

The hopper car was the major piece of EBT rolling stock. The EBT was the first narrow gauge line to acquire all-steel cars in 1913-14; it built its own steel hopper cars beginning in 1914. Hopper #1029 was part of a group of 40 cars assigned to ganister rock service, as denoted by the lettering "Rock" under the number. It is pictured at Mount Union in 1956, the final year of regular operation.

Flat car #110 was one of a dozen steel flat cars constructed by the EBT in 1923. It survived until the end of operations and is seen at Mount Union on dual gauge trackage in 1956. Flat car #106 was converted with standard gauge trucks in 1948 for use in the Mount Union yards.

Tank car #116, seen at Orbisonia in 1956, was built as a flat car in 1925 by the Orbisonia shops. A 6,000-gallon tank was added to the car in the late 1930s.

BELOW. The EBT maintained a fleet of wooden and steel box cars. Steel car #167 was built in 1920 and is shown near the Mount Union enginehouse in 1956. RIGHT. The logo of the EBT was painted on rolling stock, including elderly wooden box cars. *William S. Young*

Freshly outshopped box car #170 was constructed by the EBT in 1913. The 32′1″-long car had a steel underframe and a wooden body. It is seen at Orbisonia with fresh paint and lettering. *Joe R. Thompson*

Wooden box car #170 is seen prior to being repainted. The weathered look of the old car is probably more authentic than the new paint job since Pennsylvania winters were especially hard on wooden rolling stock, and fresh paint did not last more than a few years.

Hopper car #618 was a rare two-bay car because only four cars of this style remained after World War II. It is shown on dual gauge trackage at Mount Union in 1956.

Hopper car #960 is a typical three-bay hopper built in the EBT shops in 1917. The car has not received extended sideboards nor the company's logo.

Hopper #1000 is a three-bay 70,000-pound capacity car built by the EBT in 1918. This photo was taken in 1969.

Hopper car #1046 was one of 124 cars rebuilt with extended sideboards between 1943 and 1949. The higher sides increased carrying capacity from 70,000 to 80,000 pounds, and they were fabricated of steel in the EBT shops. Hopper car #995, coupled behind hopper car #1046, is an example of an unmodified hopper.

LEFT. The EBT built scale test car #30 in its shops in 1916. Seen here at Orbisonia, the short, 13′ 7″ car weighed 30,000 pounds. The #30 was used to test the accuracy of scales located at Robertsdale, Orbisonia and Mount Union. BELOW. The EBT operated a pair of standard gauge air-dump cars, #12 and #13, in the Mount Union yards. Note that the cars are equipped with both full-size standard gauge couplers and three-quarter-size couplers for mating with narrow gauge equipment.

The East Broad Top Railroad & Coal Co.

The EBT operated a pair of red cabooses that it built in 1920. This one is at Orbisonia in 1954, and it is in need of a coat of paint. *William S. Young*

Photographer and artist, the late Philip A. Ronfor photographed this scene that he entitled "Sunset on the Narrow Gauge" in 1955. Caboose #28, a high-sided hopper car, and combination car #14 sit near the EBT shops.

One of the reasons why the EBT lasted longer than any other narrow gauge railroad in the East was its ability to run standard gauge cars over its line without having to reload or "break-bulk." By utilizing the old timber transfer, the EBT crewmen substituted a pair of Vulcan narrow gauge trucks for those on the standard gauge car and sent it on its way down the yard-wide trackage. A unique aluminum casting compensated for the difference in coupler size and car height. The locomotive is coupled to a standard gauge car, and these trainmen admire their handiwork.

PHOTOS: LEFT, RIGHT, BOTTOM. The date is March 23, 1956, and the location is the passing siding at Adams, a few miles south of Mount Union. The train orders call for southbound #17 Extra, with several loads of company coal and empty hoppers, to pull into the siding. Meanwhile, northbound #16 Extra, with loads of ganister rock and freshly mined coal, passes on the main line. In time-honored tradition, crews of the two trains inspect the other train for defects and hot boxes. Then, the switch is thrown, and #17 Extra continues toward Orbisonia. *Philip A. Ronfor*

EBT #16 Extra North leaves Adams following the meet and continues to Mount Union with its consist of ganister rock and coal. The rock comes from the Narco Branch and is destined for the brick factories of Mount Union. Within two weeks, the final clean-up run over the narrow gauge will be made, and the EBT will shut down. *Philip A. Ronfor*

A loaded coal drag crosses Aughwick Creek trestle, near Pogue, behind 2-8-2 #16 on February 13, 1956. This trestle, with its two 105′ spans and girder approach, was the longest on the line. *William S. Young*

Combination car #14 trails a northbound freight across Aughwick Creek trestle in the autumn of 1954.

LEFT. Following the final run on April 6, 1956, the EBT was sold to the Kovalchick Salvage Company. Owner Nick Kovalchick and his family did not have the heart to tear up the historic line. They retained EBT Operating Vice President C. Roy Wilburn and others on the payroll and, on August 13, 1960, the EBT was officially re-opened on several miles of trackage north from Orbisonia. *Emery Gulash* BELOW. More equipment and trackage were restored over the next few years and, in 1964, the EBT was declared a National Historic Landmark. EBT #12 hauled passengers on the first trips over the rebuilt line and has since been joined by #14, #15 and #17. *Joe R. Thompson*

BELOW. Refinished passenger cars wait for another weekend of service at the Orbisonia depot. *Emery Gulash*